"It's not what you are that is holding you back. It's what you think you are not."

—Anonymous

WHO ARE YOU, REALLY?

The Search for Authenticity

RAY LECARA JR, MCLC

SYNER-G PUBLISHING

SEATTLE

Published in the U.S. by Syner-G Publishing, Seattle.

Publisher's Cataloging-in-Publication Data
Names: LeCara, Ray Jr., author.
Title: Who Are You, Really? The Search for Authenticity | Ray LeCara Jr
Description: Seattle, WA: Syner-G Publishing, 2022.
Identifiers: LCCN: 2022918304 | ISBN: 978-1-7379394-7-4
Subjects: LCSH Self-actualization (Psychology) | Success—Psychological aspects. | Leadership. | Conduct of life. | Stress management. | Self help. | BISAC SELF-HELP / Personal Growth / General
Classification: LCC BF637.S4 .L43 2022 | DDC 158.1--dc23

Book Jacket Design © SGP
Cover Image by John Hain (Pixabay)

Printed in the USA | Syner-GPublishing.com

First Edition

*In memory of Connie
who taught me the value of
authenticity*

ii

"When do you feel most authentic? Authenticity feels so natural, so why isn't it easy?"
— *Robert Holden*

"Being authentic begins with unconditional self-acceptance—imperfections and all."
— *Azim Jamal and Brian Tracy*

"Be so authentically you that others feel safe to be themselves too."
— *Anonymous*

iv

TABLE OF CONTENTS

INTRODUCTION

I remember the first time I read *Flow* by Mihaly Robert Csikszentmihalyi. Sadly, Csikszentmihalyi passed away a little more than a year ago at the age of 84. His book, *Flow*, was a game-changing read and it is one of the few that I pass on to people. I've even given away my paperback copies. It's that important. That amazing. Why? For me, it wasn't just how *flow*—a positive and content state of consciousness—was achievable through mindset and intention rather than the byproduct of elusive randomness, it was the way Csikszentmihalyi broke it all down. It made sense. His work communicated that *we* are in control of *our* happiness. Furthermore, reading his work, one can't help but realize it is information that should already be intrinsically known and, perhaps on some level, we are already aware of this. We just never focus on it long enough for it to help us viii

transform. Reading his book moves that process along so that every reader can begin making the necessary adjustments in their life to witness—to experience—the state of flow Csikszentmihalyi describes.

Who Are You, Really? The Search for Authenticity isn't ground-breaking. It isn't new science. Much of it is nearly common sense. Sense that we question even though we know it to be accurate or true on some level. But because we've been conditioned to focus on distractions or things that, in the end, are truly unimportant, we ignore the SELF. Even with the red flags, the discomfort, we ignore the SELF—the truth—as it applies to us. The result: profound frustration and a search for something that has been right in front of us all along.

You are important. Somewhere inside you, you know this to be true. You matter. Focusing on yourself is not narcissism. It isn't arrogance. It isn't selfishness. When flight attendants instruct passengers to apply the oxygen cup to themselves before helping others, is that act one of selfishness?

To offer your best to the world, to be real and genuine, you need to be well. You need to be well to be *your* best; to be *at* your best.

What is authenticity? What does it mean to be authentic? Dictionary.com defines authentic as "representing one's true nature or beliefs; true to oneself or to the person identified." Fitting, then, how being true to one's nature, beliefs, or oneself has never been more essential to living a life of contentment. Nor has it ever been more difficult to articulate.

The goal of *Who Are You, Really? The Search for Authenticity* is to offer some understanding of how a mindset guarded against negative thoughts and influences can transform your life, your relationships, your career, and even your learning. Chances are you already know this. The challenge, however, is achieving that mindset.

Regardless of age, the time for waiting is over. Enough with burdening yourself being all things to all people. Enough with being stuck in unfulfilling relationships or dead-end jobs. Lost? Questioning your path? Angry? Emotional? Exhausted? Unsure why but sensing there's supposed to be something more to life? These are characteristics of living inauthentically.

The time is now. *Your* time is now. If the pandemic reinforced anything it is that things can change when we least expect. And those changes are sometimes off the rails. The more grounded we are in authenticity, the easier it is to center ourselves for a return to a state of equilibrium. Of manageability. And the more fulfilling each and every blessed day can be.

Split into five chapters, this book is a fairly quick read with explanations broken down into four sections representing areas to which the chapter's message(s) can be applied: that of authentically living, loving, leading, and even learning.

Living Authentically. This section of each chapter will refer to the self. More specifically, you, the reader. The individual. Together we will explore what you can do to find—and maintain—your most authentic self. Learning to live in a way that is *true to you* is not easy. But even making progress towards this mindset is transformative.

Fallible. Human. We stumble. We fall. We make mistakes. Through these we also learn. Life is easier (not easy, but easier) when we operate from a place of genuineness. Of authenticity. Our purpose becomes clearer. Challenges are viewed differently. Life itself takes on a new meaning when at peace with oneself, when not striving to fit into someone else's mold, when not trying to be something we are not.

Loving Authentically. A fulfilling life comes from relationships, be they platonic, familial, intimate, or all of the above. And yet there is such a struggle with how to establish, nurture, maintain, and even end some of these relationships. Ambivalence holds us back from properly addressing situations, as does our lack of self and who we are. Why else would we continue to subject ourselves to toxic and unrewarding associations? Family or not, is it worth your mental health?

Leading Authentically. You don't have to be a manager, supervisor, or CEO to be a leader. You might be actively involved in your local town, school, or religious community. Maybe you are part of a department where you work. Even if you are none of these, you are still someone who can lead by example. This leading can be quiet and understated. It can be intentional and self-aware.

However intentional or unintentional, as a peer, colleague, member of a staff, group, company, or organization, you still lead. You lead by your actions—what is unspoken—and your words. You lead by example. You lead by consistency. You lead by how you respond to things and others. You lead by how you hold yourself.

What makes an effective leader? One who operates from their most authentic self.

Learning Authentically. While this section seems custom-made for young people, we are all life-long learners. Here we won't just be targeting readers who are still in school. We'll explore how Learning Authentically has as much an impact on adults as it does on young people.

Who Are You, Really? The Search for Authenticity is the beginning of your transformation. Only by peeling back the layers can you expect to access your most authentic self. The more honest you can be with yourself, the more your life will change.

"*Authenticity means erasing the gap between what you firmly believe inside and what you reveal to the outside world.*"

– Adam Grant
Author

1 Who Are You, Really?

Who are you? Who are you, really? Seems an easy enough question, right? Why, then, does such a question elicit a deer-in-headlights expression with an oft spoken response of "I don't know." Perhaps it is because not many people have taken the time to explore the question. Not fully. Not thoroughly. Sure, they may have had to think about it when completing an application for employment, a scholarship, or when preparing for an interview but that's often as far as it goes. It just isn't something that is given a priority.

And yet, what is usually the first phrase spoken by a prospective employer: "Tell me about yourself." If unprepared, how do you think most people respond? Even with practice and preparation, answers to questions such as this one can come off as disingenuous or forced. Why? Because to truly answer the question, people need to take the time to peel back the layers. It's hard to answer a question to which you are ambivalent about its answer.

So, who are you? At your core. What *defines* you? Some people are defined by a sport or activity. For others, it's their association with family or friends. Their children. Perhaps their heritage defines them. It can be a title they hold at work. Maybe something else defines them entirely or they aren't defined by anything at all yet. That's fine, too.

For others to appreciate you, there are aspects of who you are that first need acknowledging. By you! That is why it is essential to identify those things that make you who you are. Things such as your talents, skills, and passions. Even your likes, dislikes, dreams, activities, and friendships are all crucial. You may not reveal all this to a future employer or to casual friends, but YOU need to be cognizant of these attributes. When it comes to how you perceive yourself and, perhaps more importantly, how you project yourself to others, it is necessary to be aware of these personal details. Tapping into them offers you greater flexibility in multiple situations. Because so many of us are much more complex and interesting than we ever give ourselves credit for being, keeping inventory of these characteristics allows for a greater sense of self and the opportunity for deeper connections with others.

We are multi-dimensional beings. I know. I know. What does that even mean? It means there are multiple aspects to who we are. There's the physical, the emotional, the spiritual, the intellectual, and the creative. Let's dive a bit deeper into each.

The Physical. Are you an active person? If so, what do you like to do? What activities do you enjoy? Maybe your approach to living, loving, leading, and learning is very hands-on.

The Emotional. Are you someone who can empathize with others or sense people's emotions? Are you someone who "feels" more than your peers? If you are, do you hold back for fear of how your friends and family may respond? Even though free expression is championed, society seems to dictate—or wants to dictate—who is allowed to be emotional and why.

The Spiritual. Some people connect with a faith or look to nature for a sense of spirituality, belonging, and strength. This refers to our spiritual side.

The Intellectual. Those who identify with being intellectual do so because they are inquisitive about things and are always seeking answers. Curiosity drives them. Learning is important. Exciting. Whether or not they can absorb information like a sponge, some just enjoy the challenge of learning new things.

The Creative. Are you a creative person? Some love crafting stories, drawing, or writing/playing music. Some build things. Design things. They express their creativity through cooking or fashion or construction. How about you?

Take a moment to explore who you are. Do you find you are more physical than emotional? Intellectual over creative? All of the above? In what way(s)? What defines you? List the things you enjoy doing vs the things you don't. Explore why. What makes you smile? Proud? Content? How about the things that anger, frustrate, disappoint, or hurt you?

LIVING WHO YOU ARE AUTHENTICALLY

Accessing your most authentic self opens the world to new experiences and a growth mindset. This mindset embraces the challenges that come with being human and navigating everyday experiences. Live authentically and this mindset thrives because the individual, the self, is resilient. Nearly impervious to outside influences, you'll not be bullied or conned into something that is not in alignment with your authentic self.

Knowing who you are means that no one can take advantage of you. Knowing who you are means that when you get up in the morning, gone is the restlessness. Less vocal is the negative talk in your mind. Absent will be the search for what to do, who to be. You will instead be living a life of purpose. The more we know who we are, the more capable we are of doing something purpose<u>ful</u> every day besides just existing. We live. Profoundly.

The reason why so many are unhappy every day, the reason why so many individuals walk around in a daze, the reason why so many find themselves buried in destructive habits is because they don't know who they are. If they did, the path to transformation would be more accessible. More apparent.

We are surrounded by ticking time bombs—an angry, frustrated population that doesn't know how to appropriately express their emotions. Awkward in their interactions and in their own engagements, they are forever second-guessing themselves. They will react rather than respond to events, circumstances, and situations. Meaning, they will act without thinking. We see this in abundance in the aftermath of COVID because part of the populace has forgotten how to properly interact with one another. Profoundly exhausted from the last few years of isolation and uncertainty, of bottling up everything, how else to express this angst than to give in to random—sometimes uncontrolled—outbursts? This is not to excuse the behavior. Acknowledging it for what it is, however, goes far when addressing or responding to it.

Even before the pandemic wreaked havoc with social interactions, there have always been those who act out of context or utter something inappropriate to mask their awkwardness. These individuals fail to properly recognize social cues. Because they see something humorous on TikTok or YouTube, for example, they try to imitate this as a way for them to move past that awkwardness that they feel. But that wouldn't be necessary if they knew who they were.

Reflecting on who you are doesn't freeze you in time. It doesn't mean you're still not going to change. Grow. Evolve. We all do. And before social media, everyone was able to do it removed from the public eye, save for a few grainy photos or blurred videos. But self-care, self-reflection, exploring our wants, our needs, and our aspirations are the things that help foster positive growth. Before getting to that point, we first want to—*need to*—be able to acknowledge our inner nature and what makes us this way.

Where does this come from? It comes from those things that we like, those things that we're passionate about, and those things that bring a smile to our face. Just as important are those things we dislike. Those things we get caught up doing for others that make us uncomfortable or have no value because we're spinning our wheels serving someone else's dreams, whims, career move or power trip.

If you know who you are, it will be more difficult for people to exploit you because you will be too focused on *your* purpose. *Your* mission. *Your* vision. You won't be as triggered. If you're someone who gets triggered by things, you won't be *as* triggered because these things that are happening around you are not going to be as powerful or nearly as influential.

LOVING WHO YOU ARE AUTHENTICALLY

Relationships are difficult. They're difficult whether they are new and in the establishing phase or if they happen to be historical. When it's a new relationship, we want to make a good impression as we establish rapport with that other person or group. That's to be expected. It's the long-term relationships that can become much more complicated. Reflect on some of your long-term relationships. Reflect on those long-term relationships where there exists a great deal of history between you and the other person. It could be a platonic one. It can be romantic, but with a complicated history. Complications happen within our circle of family and friends with whom we've known for decades.

People grow and change, but many who have a history with you tend to remember you *as you were* rather than accepting you as you are. This is especially so if *they* have not grown or changed much. That's where being authentic comes in. Even if those around you don't understand your growth, it's not going to be as significant to you because you will be too focused on being YOU.

Finding yourself immersed in situations with friends and relatives that are toxic or triggering? Relationships and holiday event gatherings can bring about a lot of grief, strife, and drama. Knowing *who you are* makes things easier—not easy, but easier—because the resonance of these situations is often a reflection of the views and perceptions we carry of ourselves. Stepping back to view the situation objectively—responding instead of reacting—is a by-product of being comfortable with yourself. To know yourself is to be comfortable in the most awkward of situations because you will perceive things differently. You will come to comprehend why people act the way they do. That is not to excuse someone's abhorrent behavior or the words they use. But by recognizing its source we can better respond without going on the defensive. Absent will be the feeling that we're being mocked, ridiculed, intimidated, judged, or intentionally provoked. Missing will be the need to defend our ego. And if necessary, we'll have the strength to exit hostile situations, removing ourselves from those who aren't very much in alignment with their own authentic selves and who perceive lashing out as the only means to deal with their own insecurity.

When one lacks alignment, it can cause discomfort and awkwardness in the company of others who are, themselves, dealing with feelings of inadequacy. Guess what? Just so we're clear, awkwardness is all about being alive. It's what it means to be human. Embrace it. Life is full of awkward situations. Conversations are full of awkward situations.

We may trip at the worst times in front of others. We may fall. We may drop food on our shirts or enter a room with our zipper down. We want so badly to look perfect because that is what we've been conditioned to strive for. But perfection is elusive. Impossible to achieve. Online, on social media, on TV, in the movies, everybody appears picture-perfect. Even when they're supposed to be disheveled, experiencing pain, or going through a rough patch, many times their appearance is the opposite of reality.

Until that shift happens in mindset, until it is realized that one can never be perfect, or perfect enough, missed will be the moments that make us human. You see, reality is full of beautifully awkward, imperfect moments. Take, for example, dog owners. Dog owners

Ray LeCara Jr | 15

know that at some point they will have to contend with dog hair and muddy paw prints at the most inopportune times.

For couples, some of the most memorable, funniest, most endearing romantic moments are awkward ones. Consider why that might be.

We can choose to fret over these situations because of what other people may think or how they may respond, but if in alignment with our most authentic selves, suddenly those moments are not as big a deal as they used to be. They are, in fact, merely a part of life.

When it comes to fostering meaningful relationships, people are going to seek you out because you will stand strong based on who you are. Confident. Assured. Because of all that you bring to the table—as a friend, as a confidant, as someone who recognizes their strengths, their skills, accomplishments, and talents.

LEADING WHO YOU ARE AUTHENTICALLY

Knowing ourselves is vital to our employment experiences because it levels the playing field. You or someone else may hold a title, but that does not diminish anyone as an individual. As a human being. With an authentically leading mindset, you will be in a position where others will not be allowed to steal your power.

In this post-COVID time, more than ever before people are recognizing the health benefits of working to live, not necessarily living to work. Unless that is your passion or lifestyle. Unless you are the driving force behind an idea, a company, a product, or the like. What we're referring to here are those who work long hours spinning their wheels not getting any traction. Not going anywhere. Maybe this is you. Many of us have been in this situation at one time or another. Feeling that for all the effort, for all the giving and giving and giving, there is no return on that investment. It doesn't take long before resentment sets in, especially if there isn't any way to move up or forward or when someone else takes credit for your efforts—your unappreciated efforts. Once more, this is where being connected to your authentic self can be beneficial.

When you are authentically aligned, you will be more aware and readily able to pick up on something that is amiss. Furthermore, you won't let it continue. Authenticity lets you be candid with your co-workers or your employer. Not in a rude or condescending way, either. It's about awakening to those who abuse your sincerity, drown out your voice, and place themselves in a position to step all over you.

Early on in a career or when first starting at a place of employment, it is not uncommon to put up with certain things when new, to get ahead, or to become established. This makes sense. Everyone needs to earn their place. But some will put up with too much even as red flags are apparent the longer they remain where they are. Only later, sometimes with experience, sometimes with age, sometimes with both, do we take a stand realizing it's not worth it. Life is about working your way up, earning your stripes. But that doesn't mean having to debase yourself, watching it happen to others, or becoming a sycophant to maintain a position.

When you truly know who you are then you become aware that the stress that's present from not being authentic rarely originates from you anymore. It's often co-workers and those in a leadership position who are the miserable ones. They become indifferent when not recognized, acknowledged, or if they are feeling underappreciated and taken for granted. Yet it isn't just their peers or the place of employment failing to recognize them. Many times *they* don't acknowledge their own strengths, talents, and accomplishments. They become envious of those they see succeeding or perhaps getting more attention for doing less. They then lead by fear. Feeling threatened by those around them, they fail to recognize the value in uplifting the others. Supporting them. Empowering them. Instead, they do the opposite. Everything becomes a power play.

Offering an employee more money cannot fix or resolve these issues. Studies show that employees don't leave their jobs as much for the money as for the respect, dignity, and acknowledgement with which they should be afforded. According to Leigh Branham, author of *The 7 Hidden Reasons Employees Leave*, management still has no clue. Branham notes how nearly 90 percent of employers are convinced employees exit because of salary issues when it's quite the opposite. Just over ten percent leave in search of more money.

True leaders demonstrate. They model. Their actions match their words. They are all about successfully upleveling those around them even if it means these employees leave the organization. As a March 2018 Forbes.com article notes, based on studies conducted globally, "nothing else comes close to recognition—not even higher pay, promotion, autonomy or training."

Happy people don't leave companies. They become loyal and care just as much about the brand.

On the next page, reflect on how you live, love, and/or lead authentically. If you endeavor to be more authentic in any of these areas, make note of it. Be honest with yourself. Why? What do you think is missing? What do you hope to transform in these areas?

**Take this chapter one step further. Consider Mind Mapping the reflective areas of this chapter, especially if you are a visual person. You can find out more about Mind Mapping on page 120.

Living Who You Are Authentically

Loving Who You Are Authentically

Leading Who You Are Authentically

"*Everyone wants to matter. They want respect from peers and recognition for their accomplishments. Not out of vanity or selfishness, but of an earnest desire to fulfill a personal potential.*"

–Ryan Holiday
Author

2 Living Up to Your Potential

E ver feel as if you are not living up to your potential? Ever wonder just what your potential is? Discovering this—exploring this—through your authentic self serves many purposes.

Being true to yourself is directly connected to your sense of well-being, overall identity, and your happiness. How can one expect to be happy if they are forced to be something that doesn't reflect who they are at their core? According to Dr. Bruce Lipton, an American developmental biologist, "Many people sabotage themselves 95% of the day. Why? It is because they are struggling to reprogram how they were taught to think and view the world around them."

Whether through being, doing, or speaking, staying true to yourself will keep you from getting caught up in whatever is part of the zeitgeist at the moment. Trends and fads, don't forget, come and go. Now is the time to assess what you're capable of by taking the time to know yourself.

Where to begin? First, work through the first chapter. Next, check out some of the personality tests listed on pages 137 and 138. These assessments are free. Understand they do not diagnose in any way, but they do offer insight and a starting point for reflection, conversation, and action.

Use this area to record your thoughts ahead of or after trying out the personality tests. Perhaps you've taken them before. Do it once more. Compare what's remained the same with what has changed. Consider how you can begin to use the information you've learned.

To best reflect on our potential, it makes sense to investigate that which makes us who we are at this moment. Peeling back those layers, for some, may be difficult. Statistically speaking, some may have a family, a home, a certain number of automobiles, a certain number of children. A title. High paying job. Maybe they coach. Belong to the Rotary Club. Volunteer often within the community. Attend the local church. Everything looks perfect. *On paper.* But these very same individuals may be miserable compared to those who seemingly have nothing that resembles success and yet are happy. Happier. Think about why that might be. Think about why society—along with advertising and social media—seems to work so hard at convincing individuals in these more modest situations that they, too, *should be* just as miserable. Especially if they're not striving for the same material goals or symbols of success as their contemporaries.

Where, then, does the misery come from? Zig Ziglar, an American author and motivational speaker once noted that "Far too many people have no idea of what they *can do* because all they have been told is what they *can't do*. They don't know what they want because they don't know what's available for them." Too often, the discontent detected coming from someone else is misdirected. It could be a situation that occurred at home growing up with siblings and parents. It could be an unresolved issue that occurred at school that still eats away at the heart. Regret. Lack of connections. Misery can percolate from soured relationships since early on they can shape our perception of friendship and relationships, even views on intimacy and sex. Whether it looks on paper as if they have it all or not, people are miserable for several reasons. The one that stands out the most? It is centered around the self.

So much of what an individual battles throughout life originates from their sense of self. Therefore, accessing who you are is the first step towards addressing some of those unresolved conflicts and perceptions. Feeling as if you've missed out on something? Feeling you've been wronged? These are very human ways to perceive things. But that may not reflect truth. A distorted or unrealized sense of self is limiting. It limits one from achieving success, happiness, peace, and contentment.

In early 2022, American investor, billionaire, and Warren Buffet's business partner for over 40 years, Charlie Munger, 98, claimed that society doesn't have so much a greed problem as an envy problem. That "envy" is borne out of discontent. It is what happens when negative-speak infects one's thoughts. The feeling of having missed something, currently missing things, or the possibility of missing out on something can easily lead to guilt, regret, resentment, and anger. Most are happy for your success so long as your success does not eclipse their own. And be prepared for friends and strangers to exhibit noticeably different behavior if you decide to go against the norm in pursuit of your dreams, your happiness, your authenticity.

A musician client of mine didn't realize he really wanted to pursue music when he was younger. But whatever he was doing at the time he graduated high school allowed him to jump right into earning money. Who isn't excited at the prospect of making a good check at a young age?

And yet that's how we get swept up into forgoing our own dreams because we think that with enough money we can then begin that path to having what everyone else has, doing what everyone else is doing.

Years later when that same job is no longer fulfilling because it does not actually align with your authentic self, it can be earth shattering. Why? Marriage. Mortgage. Bills. A roof overhead. Mouths to feed. Some are dealing with it all. As an already established adult, it's difficult to transition to something else, authentic or not, because of the many responsibilities that are firmly in place. But that doesn't mean it is impossible. It's just not something that can happen overnight. It will require steps to transition to something more in alignment. Something that *feels* right. Makes you happier. Perhaps more whole. Something that allows you to live up to your potential *and* pays the bills.

To begin living up to your potential, you first need to take stock of who you are *now*. Working with people through coaching, I find it takes about four to six sessions for people to begin to trust. This is based on consistency— how they show up, and how they feel about their coach and about themselves. That last one can be the trickiest. Transformation begins with transforming one's mindset. It's not a one-and-done deal. There are no quick fixes. It is not the place of the coach to *tell* clients what to do. The answer lies within the client. Deep within. The learning comes with—and from—the journey. Even this publication. I don't doubt there will be many ah-ha moments for readers. But a single reading won't bring overnight changes. Know that one still needs to put in the work. Work through the exercises here. Then as you begin that internal journey, seek out those who can further that along. A mentor. A coach. An open and available friend or relative.

The transition is gradual. It takes some time for it to be real. Authentic, if we want to be wholly honest with ourselves. Discovering your potential means you first have to put aside that time. Be ready to invest. To reflect. To take action. With that investment will come the belief in yourself and your many incredible abilities.

LIVING UP TO YOUR POTENTIAL AUTHENTICALLY

Are you happy? To understand if you're living up to your potential, this question comes into play. If you feel that you are living up to your potential, then chances are you're going to answer that you are happy. That doesn't mean there aren't unfinished things that you have in play or in mind. But it has to do with your mindset. It has to do with gratitude. It has to do with living each day with purpose.

There is something missing when we are given things without having earned them. By putting in the work, by exploring and going through that journey to discover our most authentic self, the time and effort behind that journey means we will have earned the information sought after for so long: what we are capable of *and* what is possible.

LOVING UP TO YOUR POTENTIAL AUTHENTICALLY

Most if not all relationships, I would argue, are grounded in love. Allow yourself to be authentic and you will find that there is an abundance of love when it comes to being around other people, regardless of gender. Age. Regardless of blood. Know that this mindset does not mean you're going to love everybody that you encounter. Furthermore, that "love" can merely be the euphoric feeling that you get by being around—or with— others who value you as much as you value them. Perhaps it will come from establishing relationships as part of an unexplained deeply rooted connection. But the love that is felt during these moments explains more about how *you* process that moment—the gratitude for the experiences, the connection, and the value you are given equaling the value you give others.

Living up to your potential when it comes to love has much to do with the relationships that you cultivate. In a 2021 poll of 1100 people by StudyFinds.org, 91 percent of those surveyed admitted they find conversations "bore them." Since discussions today are often not true conversations (an exchange of thoughts and feelings between people), why wouldn't they be boring?

Think about your exchanges. How often do those discussions tend to be deep? Sadly, conversations—even with people we've known for years—are often generic in topic. Superficial. Safe. Especially in recent years when politics or issues of controversy cannot be discussed because of their divisiveness. The result: cancelation. But there is still so much more we can discuss, however, if we're being authentic and focusing on the individual.

When we retread, when we regurgitate, when we revisit the same topics over and over and over and over, it is for this reason that so many do not enjoy conversation. If they only knew that when we are all at our most authentic that the potential to learn something new becomes a game-changer. The expectation, then, is that everyone comes to the conversation ready to participate, listening as much as sharing.

> *"74% of people hate their job… The majority of people don't like what they're doing. You have to have a purpose no matter what you do in life. Don't be afraid of failing. We all fail. It's okay. What's not okay is when you fail and you stay down."*
> —Arnold Schwarzenegger

LEADING UP TO YOUR POTENTIAL AUTHENTICALLY

To lead is not an easy job. It takes a special kind of person to be a leader. Know this: The purpose of a true leader—an authentic leader—is to inspire. An authentic leader encourages. Uplifts others. In the workplace, a leader who takes on those characteristics is going to do everything they can to see that others achieve their... wait for it... POTENTIAL! They don't hold anyone back. They don't wait for their colleagues, their peers, their employees, their staff to speak up because the reality is, on their own, they hardly do. Most don't want the attention and easily embarrass. Yet just a little acknowledgement, a little private, sincere, authentic recognition, can go so far.

Employees at most jobs are willing to remain, even for less pay, if they are acknowledged and appreciated. These gestures help signal to employees that they are working at or towards their potential. Workers will defer additional pay and even advancement if they feel fulfilled in the position that they're in. But too many leaders do not know how to lead. They've gotten into a position because of convenience. Because of timing. Sometimes it is because of whatever they bring to the table. But education and experience do not make a leader. Over half the managers in a 2018 CareerBuilder.com study admitted that "they didn't receive *any* management training... on *how* to lead." They were promoted based on their productiveness and knowledge, not the essential management and guidance skills needed to empower, inspire, and motivate those they've been chosen to lead.

While leaders may know much about the job, performance, or whatever that specific career area of expertise happens to be, the most effective and impactful leaders are selfless in their contributions to both the organization and their peers. They are someone who puts their clients, students, or patients first. These attributes come from someone who is self-assured. It is a person willing to make mistakes. Willing to own up to them because they believe the strength of the place they work at comes from serving as an example, thus uplifting, supporting, and encouraging others around them to soar even if it means they might someday move on within or outside the company.

True leaders do not wait for those under them to jump up and down to draw attention to something that they've accomplished. True leaders are going to go out of their way to recognize what others do (their successes, their accomplishments—however great or small), and how they make the business look good.

Those are real and true leaders. One ends up reaching potential as a leader when helping others reach theirs. The more that you can put yourself in the shoes of your peers, your colleagues, your department, your employees, the more effective leader you will be. It is a trait lost on some modern-day leaders who forget what it's like to be a new employee or working in challenging positions—perhaps one the leader vacated.

The more you know yourself, the more you will be able to recognize your strengths and what strengths others come ready to share. As a leader, surround yourself with that mindset. Acknowledge that the people around you have their strengths, and those strengths may exceed yours in certain areas. That does not detract from your ability to lead. By embracing this mindset, this practice, you become an even more effective and powerful leader. More importantly, you become a role model. And that helps you reach your potential because you're not just impacting your department or your coworkers, you're impacting those who go on and who never forget the examples you set, what you did, and how you made them feel.

LEARNING UP TO YOUR POTENTIAL AUTHENTICALLY

If we want to reach our potential as learners, we need to look at where our strengths lie. What are *your* strengths as a learner? What areas of *your* learning would be considered works in progress? To reach our potential when it comes to further education and learning, we need to look at not just who we are as individuals, we need to look at who we are as learners.

The more authentic we are about what we know and don't know, the easier it will be for us to overcome influences that steer us astray. Like the adage implies, knowledge *IS* power. Knowing how and when to learn is just as important as the learning itself. Knowledge uplevels you. Knowledge protects you. Knowledge helps you recognize truth in a world of lies and misdirects.

In education, in the academic environment, knowing who you are will help you discover purpose through acknowledging those things that are of interest to you. Learners feel lost in school, disconnected, because many only know the purpose of education as something that must be completed. Yes, it is recognized to be the path to college and hopefully a prosperous career. But that's not happening if you don't know *why* you're going to school or if you are randomly picking a path because that's what you've been told to do. How can one expect to reach their potential if they are forced to pursue something that has no internal connection, no meaning, or lacks interest?

If you would like to discover how you think and learn best, consider taking the Multiple Intelligences assessment on page 138. There you will also find a Career assessment. Once you've addressed the exercises in the first two chapters, and you're looking for how to reach your potential as a learner, this is the next step towards achieving your authentic learning potential.

_____

Reflect on your potential in the areas of living, loving, leading, and/or learning authentically. What do you think is missing? What do you hope to transform?

Living Up to Your Potential Authentically

Loving Up to Your Potential Authentically

Leading Up to Your Potential Authentically

Learning Up to Your Potential Authentically

Additional Take-Aways/Notes

"THERE IS NO HEAVIER BURDEN THAN AN UNFULFILLED POTENTIAL."
—CHARLES SCHULZ

www.social-anxiety-solutions.com

"Authenticity is everything! You have to wake up every day and look in the mirror, and you want to be proud of the person who's looking back at you. And you can only do that if you're being honest with yourself."

– Aaron Rodgers
NFL Quarterback

3 Vulnerability & Transparency

To be authentic we need to be willing to be both vulnerable *and* transparent. This doesn't mean vulnerable to the point of allowing others to harm or hurt us but vulnerable enough to be willing to go beyond the superficial to engage in more meaningful conversations and experiences.

The more authentic a person is, the more transparent that person will be. And by transparency we mean honesty. Sincereness. Admitting fault when wrong. An admiral trait since what we see isn't always what is happening. It is so very easy to jump to conclusions. If we're going to aspire to be transparent, if we're going to allow ourselves to be vulnerable, we first need to make sure we're aware of what the "rules" are and what the expectations are for everyone involved.

Good communication can't be something that's just talked about. It must be practiced. We cannot jump to conclusions. When authentic in all areas of your life, there's less worry about transparency. Because if you're going to live your life from a place of being real, genuine, and authentic, you will already be transparent.

There isn't an anxious desire to hide, cover-up, lie, or aggressively defend yourself when authentic. You're not going to feel guilt for something you didn't do. That begins to fade with the proper mindset. And you will be comfortable sharing your side of a story or situation, even if it puts you in an unflattering light. Why? Because you are coming from a place of authenticity.

Consider social media interactions. Some who are on Facebook, for example, get upset when their birthdays or posts go unacknowledged. In this situation, there may be limited responses from "friends" because the post or special event may not have been seen. Individual users may have been very focused on their own stuff. Chances are they became overwhelmed with all the other posts and notifications. It is easy to overlook the important ones because they sometimes can and do get buried.

What about the posters, though? Part of their frustration stems from making themselves vulnerable by posting anything at all. They are waiting for that recognition, that validation. If only they realized that it is very common not to get many likes or comments. If only they posted authentically, pleased if it gains a response but not devastated if it doesn't.

LIVING AUTHENTICALLY TRANSPARENT AND VULNERABLE

To be transparent and vulnerable in your everyday life means being present and open to experiences. It means allowing yourself to emotionally take in those experiences. If these experiences bring you great joy, it's okay to share with others that you find yourself emotional. It's okay to cry if experiences sadden you, outrage you, or trigger you. You have permission to reveal your sensitive side. To let it out when you need to—privately or in the presence of others.

For situations where you find yourself among others discussing something inappropriate or troublesome with no way to excuse yourself from it, then once more give yourself permission. This time it is permission to be transparent and vulnerable by admitting you are not comfortable. That you would prefer to move on in the conversation to discuss something else.

LOVING AUTHENTICALLY TRANSPARENT AND VULNERABLE

What is it that you're looking for in an acquaintance? What is it you look for in a close friend, a bestie? When dating? Make a list of the things that *you bring* to each type of relationship. How about what *you expect* in return?

ACQUAINTANCES

List everything you bring to a casual friendship

What do you expect from someone else?

CLOSE (BFF) FRIENDSHIPS

List everything you bring to a close friendship

What do you expect from someone else?

Why should any of this matter?

DATING/ROMANTIC RELATIONSHIPS

What do you bring to the relationship?	What do you expect from someone else in the relationship?

LEADING AUTHENTICALLY TRANSPARENT AND VULNERABLE

Being vulnerable and transparent when it comes to leadership means admitting when you're wrong. It also means recognizing that others may be stronger than you are in some areas. But that's not necessarily an affront to your leadership. It doesn't slight your accomplishments, nor does it diminish in any way who you are—as a person and as a leader. Nothing about it threatens your position unless you allow it to or make it an issue.

It is not uncommon for organizations and companies to protect their core values when hiring. Core values are just as important within our inner circle of friends and relationships as they are when it comes to leadership, or the work environment. Keeping this in mind when hiring will reduce the time for new hires and already established employees to bond because of similar expectations, work ethic, and mindset.

Being vulnerable in a leadership position, even as a coworker, means you are empathetic to what others experience. Take the issue of Diversity, Equity, Inclusion, and Belonging (DEIB). For all the training that has been conducted in recent years, working with all involved to be their most authentic would not only serve to reveal the internal source of resistance and lack of compassion one may have towards others, but it might also help foster a greater sense of community. A better sense of community is a sure way to promote enhanced collaboration because of everyone's comfort level, thus leading to even greater productivity due to being more aligned with the self, the surrounding team, and the company's core values. Imagine that!

LEARNING AUTHENTICALLY TRANSPARENT AND VULNERABLE

A transparent and vulnerable learner is aware of what they know and what they don't. Some of the most difficult things for learners to admit is when they don't know something or, even more frustrating, don't know *how* to learn. How to study. Let's try to de-mystify this.

Many of us are too tactical when we need to also be strategic. Tactical actions are necessary but without reflection they easily become busy work. Regardless of age or field, there are multiple benefits to stepping back and assessing *where* you are, in addition to *who* you are.

Businesses that are entirely tactical or utilize a more tactical approach might think they're taking the appropriate steps to help their business. Upon reflection, their tactical gestures of making calls and broad moves actually risk attracting clientele because of the desperation to generate income. A strategic approach, on the other hand, involves assessing tactical moves for effectiveness, progress, and whether, if any, further training is needed or an entirely different marketing approach.

A survey conducted in 2019 by the Pragmatic Institute of over 2000 professionals revealed dissatisfaction in how their time was distributed. In this survey, it was revealed that 73% of their time was being spent on tactical moves whereas only 27% was dedicated towards a strategic approach. Furthermore, those surveyed believed upwards of 53% of their time ought to be spent on strategic activities.

In education, tactical efforts might equate to completing assignments for credit but without an equally strategic approach, it becomes easy to lose sight of what the assignments are for. What was learned? Why is it important to the age group? Was it understood and what questions remain? Is further clarification necessary? What are the teacher's expectations? How are learners graded? What determines success?

A strategic approach is just as important as the tactical. Everything (and everyone) benefits from a strategic approach since it is about reflecting on the tactical moves. Whether in the academic space, at a place of employment, or within our own personal lives, regularly questioning details to better understand new incoming information is not a sign of weakness. It is a sign of strength. Instead of just "doing" something, reflecting on it leads to new ideas and a deeper level of comprehension. In some cases, it may even save you money.

Questions in a corporate environment when taking a strategic approach: Do we have a product or service that is in demand? How do we know it? What is our marketing strategy? Is it effective? Affordable? What more does the sales force need to know to authentically speak about the company and what it offers? Do the employees feel like they know what they are doing? Do they feel appreciated? Connected? Comfortable to ask questions or certain who to reach out to in all matters? Do they know what is expected and how to get ahead?

When it comes to authentically learning something, anything, it means being vulnerable and transparent about speaking up, asking questions, and gauging understanding.

The vulnerability in learning is being able to admit you're not sure how to do something. To be transparent means having to look at oneself honestly. There needs to exist a willingness to bring in others or come up with a plan, to manage time, to guard the mood, to prevent any triggers or distractions. To create boundaries, if necessary.

Reflect on how—and if—you are authentically transparent and vulnerable in the areas of living, loving, leading, and learning. What do you think is missing? What do you hope to transform?

Living Authentically Transparent
and Vulnerable

Loving Authentically Transparent
and Vulnerable

Leading Authentically Transparent
and Vulnerable

Learning Authentically Transparent
and Vulnerable

Additional Take-Aways/Notes

"*Authenticity is not needing external approval to feel good about your actions.*"

— Anonymous

4 The Most Powerful Version of You

Close your eyes. Inhale deeply. Hold your breath while you count to five. Exhale slowly. Now, write in the box below what you are grateful for at this very moment.

The most powerful version of you comes from being authentically grateful for something each and every day. The most powerful version of you also comes from knowing three important things: what it is that you *want*, *need*, and *yearn* for. Use the boxes below to explore those three areas.

What is it that you WANT... in your life? Out of life?

What is it that you **NEED**… to live… to be
happy… to feel at peace? To feel accomplished?

What is it that you **YEARN** for? Wish for? Aspire to? Desire… especially if finances weren't a concern?

To live the most powerful version of yourself is to embrace your authenticity. It's where you can find contentment. Peace. Bliss. The more authentic you are, the more you can begin enjoying life the way it's meant to be enjoyed because you will no longer be bound to the other parts of your life that only bring about negativity and depression, or exposure to toxic situations and relationships. You don't need things in your life that bring you down. That make you feel insignificant. Worthless. But you already know that. So why do you continue to put yourself in those situations, surrounding yourself with people who clearly don't value you or appreciate you for who you are?

To be the most powerful version of you authentically will take some reflection. It will take a new mindset and it will require some planning.

LIVING THE MOST POWERFUL VERSION OF YOU AUTHENTICALLY

You can—and will—find and experience peace and contentment by living your life unapologetically. That's it. Finding bliss comes from living the most powerful version of oneself authentically, less concerned about what other people think, independent of a cell phone, and free of whatever social media platform has its greatest hold. Establishing a life beholden to no one is the secret.

What is it you want *out of* your life? What is it that you want *from* life? What is it that you need? What is it that you yearn for? To achieve the most powerful version of you in those areas begins with managing your life and your time so that you always have a chance to recharge, remaining strong enough to pursue your dreams, your passions, and valued relationships. Knowing, having, or working towards your Authentic Purpose will give you what you need to ignore distractions, naysayers, block out negative thoughts, and even resist temptation from powerful influences.

You already answered the questions having to do with what it is you want, need, and yearn for. But to better articulate these answers, let's break them down for each section. Allow yourself some reflection time to complete these, even if your responses overlap or repeat.

As it pertains to Authentic Living, what is it that you want… in your life/out of life… to achieve the most powerful version of you?

As it pertains to Authentic Living, what is it
that you need... to live... to be confident...
happy... to feel at peace/content... to achieve
the most powerful version of you?

As it pertains to Authentic Living, what is it that you yearn for/wish for/desire... especially if finances weren't a concern... to achieve the most powerful version of you?

LOVING THE MOST POWERFUL VERSION
OF YOU AUTHENTICALLY

Relationships. What do you want out of love? What do you need from a friendship? There's always a honeymoon period when it comes to relationships, right? What if it was possible for relationships, no matter the kind it is you are seeking, to become deeper and more meaningful over time?

Those who have experienced it can tell you. For many, it's about sharing the most powerful version of themselves. But it's also about extracting the same from others. You're not going to be able to find that unless you are authentic or accessing some part of your authentic self. And authentic means doing the type of inventory discussed in the first chapter. This includes examining the things that bring happiness, the things that bring about a smile, the things that elicit joy. If ANY kind of relationship takes that away, then there's a problem with that relationship.

Casual. Romantic. Doesn't matter. There's never a reason to settle. You're limiting yourself, your experiences, and your interactions with that kind of thinking. Like with leadership qualities detailed earlier, true friends—true partners—empower, support, motivate, and inspire. Without them in your life, you're holding back from who you want to be or who you are. They are there. You just need to do the work to find them.

Families consist of some very interesting dynamics. Parents, for example, may have unrealistic expectations about who they want you to be—no matter how young or old you are—based entirely on their *own* perceptions. Based on their own way of looking at the world. Their experiences. It may even be cultural. But chances are it originates from how *they feel* about themselves, how *they* perceive the world, and whether they know who *they* are.

What do *you* want, need, and yearn for when it comes to relationships? When it comes to love? Friends? Family?

As it pertains to Authentic Loving, what is it that you **WANT**... in relationships/out of your relationships... to achieve the most powerful version of you?

As it pertains to Authentic Loving, what is it that you **NEED**... to feel whole... to feel/be confident in your relationships... interactions... to achieve the most powerful version of you?

As it pertains to Authentic Loving, what is it that you **YEARN** for in relationships? Wish for? Desire… especially if finances weren't a concern… to achieve the most powerful version of you?

LEADING THE MOST POWERFUL VERSION
OF YOU AUTHENTICALLY

What do you want out of the leadership positions that you're in? What do you want out of where you work as a colleague? A co-worker? The most powerful version of ourselves at work is best revealed when work doesn't feel like work. Where it is purposeful not pointless. As stated earlier, it also has to do with whether we are acknowledged. Seen. Respected. Even appreciated.

Like in families, there are people in companies and organizations that do *everything*. These individuals step up to do all the work, or most of the work, and yet it's the group that gets thanked. Everybody in the committee or department gets the Gold Star, the special treat. That can turn workers off from ever doing anything again when these situations occur. But uncovering the most powerful version of you in leadership is about living by example. Doing things regardless of recognition. It's about doing things because you choose to do them.

Are you doing what you love? Do you derive satisfaction from what you do at work? Are you passionate about it? Is it a job, a career, a lifestyle? Does the pay match your education, your knowledge, your responsibilities? Does it match your passion, your curiosity, your desire to know, learn, and become more? Is anything holding you back? What do you want, need, and yearn for when it comes to leading? When it comes to work? Your career? Job? Position?

As it pertains to Authentic Leading, what is it that you **WANT**… in your career/out of where you work… to achieve the most powerful version of you?

As it pertains to Authentic Leading, what is it that you **NEED**... to thrive... to be confident... to feel purposeful... to be happy at your job/content... to achieve the most powerful version of you?

As it pertains to Authentic Leading, what is it that you **YEARN** for at your job? Wish for a career path? Desire to be doing once you earn a suitable income… to achieve the most powerful version of you?

LEARNING THE MOST POWERFUL VERSION OF YOU AUTHENTICALLY

When it comes to learning, the most powerful version of you will own that knowledge, be it book smarts or street smarts. There is an added confidence that comes with possessing a working knowledge of something you're good at. It complements the confidence already in place from the connection you have to your true self. As a life-long learner, you endeavor to improve, to go above and beyond.

What do you want out of school? Or that class? That workshop? You may want to go into a certain kind of field. Improve what you already know. Learn the latest changes or updates. Be inspired by new ideas. Great! What do you need to make that happen? It's not uncommon for some young learners to graduate early because they are armed with the knowledge behind what they want, need, and aspire to be. What about you?

As it pertains to Authentic Learning, what is it that you **WANT**... in school/out of education? Out of further education? Workshops... to achieve the most powerful version of you?

As it pertains to Authentic Learning, what is it that you **NEED**… to learn best… to be confident that you know how to study and process new information… to achieve the most powerful version of you?

As it pertains to Authentic Learning, what is it
that you **ASPIRE** to be with your education?
Wish for as a result of your learning? Desire…
when it comes to life-long learning, especially if
finances weren't a concern… to achieve the
most powerful version of you?

Reflect on the most authentically powerful version of you overall in the areas of living, loving, leading, and learning. What might the whole package look like? How might you be there now? If you endeavor to be more authentic in any of these areas, make note of it. Be honest with yourself. What do you think is missing? What do you hope to transform?

Living Authentically Transparent and Vulnerable

Loving Authentically Transparent and Vulnerable

Leading Authentically Transparent
and Vulnerable

Learning Authentically Transparent and Vulnerable

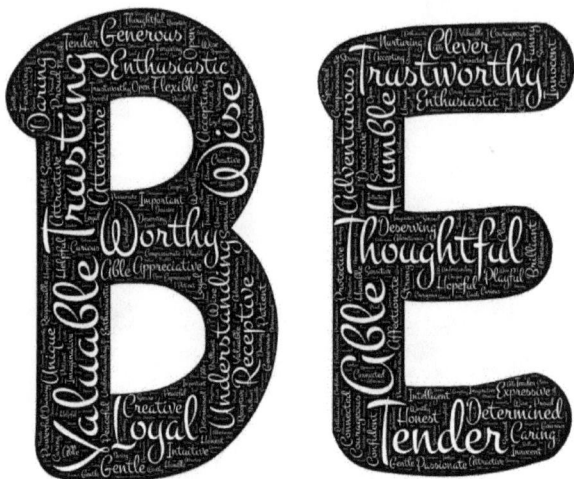

"We need to find the courage to say NO to the things and people that are not serving us if we want to rediscover ourselves and live our lives with authenticity."

—Barbara de Angelis
Spiritual Teacher

5 Authentic, Out Loud!

Topics. Strengths. Accomplishments. Talents. It's time to dispel with any aspersions—personal or otherwise—for being confident enough to put yourself out there. You've already used the previous chapters to start on the path to discovering your most authentic self. Now it's time to take it even further. To BE Authentic, Out Loud! In effect, to clearly state wherever you go, in your verbal and nonverbal cues, that *this is me!* People pick up on that. People respect that.

Whether with strangers, family, peers, co-workers, or people you are meeting for the first time, you will be able to engage on another level because of the comfort you are beginning to feel. A level of comfort that comes from no longer feeling lost, less secure, or having to be someone else.

Let's examine topics that *you* like to talk about. Consider the activity from Chapter 1. One of the easiest, most organic ways to celebrate being Authentic, Out Loud, is to engage in conversations about things that are of value and interest to you. Sure, there is small talk that some are hesitant to engage in, but small talk is really about engaging in safe and neutral topics—weather, sports, work, music, kids, and pets—that are best used to begin or initiate conversations. Once you begin to sense the other person in the conversation values you as much as you value them, that you are comfortable discussing topics that are authentically interesting or of worth to you is a game-changer. All conversations are a stepping point. Sometimes topics stick. Sometimes they are bridges to even more interesting, deeper conversations.

What's at the heart of the things that you really enjoy talking about? Consider coming up with a running list of topics that fall under the categories of living (personal, self), loving (relationships, family), leading (work, volunteerism, career goals), and learning (college major, factoids, stats). Topics that might be an extension of safer and more neutral topics. Perhaps topics that will at some point allow you to go beyond the superficial. Below are some examples.

- **Category:** Living
  - **Topics**
    - sharing what you appreciate or are grateful for
    - something about a certain season and how it might invigorate you
  - **Examples of what might be said**
    - *"I love that I get to walk my dog at the park most days before or after work."*
    - *"There's something about being on the water that is mesmerizing."*

- ➢ **Category:** Loving
  - • **Topics**
    - o something you look forward to during the holidays as it relates to family and friends
  - • **Examples of what might be said**
    - o *"Even if I don't have time to make enough to give away, I make a batch of sugar cookies because it reminds me of my grandmother."*

- ➢ **Category:** Leading
  - • **Topics**
    - o recent promotion or goal you're working towards
  - • **Examples of what might be said**
    - o *"I enjoy where I work but I see it as a steppingstone for what I truly want to do."*

- ➢ **Category:** Learning
  - • **Topics**
    - o maybe you sing or play an instrument or desire to learn something new
    - o maybe you wish to return to school, or you reflect on a deeper understanding of something learned years ago
    - o topics here can/may bleed in from other areas.
  - • **Examples of what might be said**
    - o *"I always look forward to lunch because my peers always have something new and cool to share."*

Now it's your turn.

TOPICS

LIVING Authentically, Out Loud!

LOVING Authentically, Out Loud!

LEADING Authentically, Out Loud!

LEARNING Authentically, Out Loud!

Strengths. What do you feel are your strengths? It might be your patience. Perhaps it is your ability to always be there for someone. Maybe you have the stomach to assist an ailing person or pet when they're sick.

Consider coming up with a running list of strengths that fall under the categories of living (personal, self), loving (relationships, family), leading (work, volunteerism, career goals), and learning (college major, factoids, stats). Strengths that you don't have to proclaim to the world but should be mindful of because it is an extension of who you are, were, or want to be. Below are some examples.

- ➤ **Category:** Living
  - • **Example of what could be shared**
    - ○ *"I am organized and prefer to plan things ahead of time."*

- ➤ **Category:** Loving
  - • **Example of what could be shared**
    - ○ *"I like treating my friends and family to special moments throughout the year*

instead of just on holidays or special occasions."

➢ **Category:** Leading
- **Example of what could be shared**
  - ○ *"I make a point to model what I say, even as a co-worker."*

➢ **Category:** Learning
- **Example of what could be shared**
  - ○ *"I don't like not knowing things. I prefer to research an answer before having to ask someone for help or clarification."*

Now it's your turn.

STRENGTHS

LIVING Authentically, Out Loud!

LOVING Authentically, Out Loud!

LEADING Authentically, Out Loud!

LEARNING Authentically, Out Loud!

Accomplishments. What are your triumphs? Your successes? Your achievements? If you are going to be Authentic, Out Loud, consider those things you are proud of. We're not talking about curing cancer here, though that would definitely be something to be proud of at any time. But maybe you taught yourself coding. Maybe you worked your way up to Department Chair. Maybe you bowled a perfect game. Whether you are 14 or 45, regardless of age, understand that you have accomplished A LOT!

Not sure of what you've accomplished? Ask a teacher, relative, or a friend. Parents often remember things that we forget or didn't pay much attention to. It's because we too often overlook our accomplishments, especially if we're not the type to draw attention to ourselves. Furthermore, some of these things don't *feel* like accomplishments because they came naturally or organically.

Meaning, it wasn't something you were working hard to achieve. Regardless of how easy or organically something came to you, acknowledging the accomplishment is important when it comes to one's sense of self. They are also noteworthy things to share when connecting with others and when interviewing because not everyone has accomplished what you have. They might even be strengths in the eyes of others, especially if they complement a job, position, activity, or sport that is of interest. Keep in mind that while some of your achievements may not be a big deal to you or may have come easy, not everyone can or will do what you have.

Accomplishments can be anything from learning the multiplication tables early to reading a full-length novel for the first time. Maybe you learned penmanship earlier than your peers, scored a game-winning point, or wrote your first piece of music at a young age.

Maybe you were recognized by your peers, church, or community. Maybe you filled in for a parent and raised your siblings or adopted a rescue to give it a better life. Consider maintaining a running list, starting with the one you create here. Below are some additional examples.

➢ **Category:** Living
- **Example of what could be shared**
  - ○ *"Balanced my first checkbook when I was a freshman in high school."*

➢ **Category:** Loving
- **Example of what could be shared**
  - ○ *"Sadie and I have been together for ten years."*

➢ **Category:** Leading
- **Example of what could be shared**
  - ○ *"I made sure the committee knew how appreciated they were for their hard work and effort each year with a catered lunch."*

➢ **Category:** Learning
- **Example of what could be shared**
  - ○ *"I learned HTML while everyone else was playing video games."*

Now it's your turn.

ACCOMPLISHMENTS

LIVING Authentically, Out Loud!

LOVING Authentically, Out Loud!

LEADING Authentically, Out Loud!

LEARNING Authentically, Out Loud!

Talents. What talents or skills do you possess? Maybe you play the piano. Maybe you're good at a sport, playing an instrument, learning a language quickly. Maybe you're a strong communicator or happen to be good at solving problems.

To be Authentic, Out Loud is to embrace who you truly are and to be proud of your gifts. In conversation, people have difficulty communicating with others because they feel insignificant. They feel like the person next to them has done so much more or is considerably accomplished and is, therefore, more talented. The truth is that while those around you may have succeeded at something, so have you.

Part of the reason why we make note of our talents is to have something to share when in the same room with others who are sharing theirs. It doesn't have to be an interview. This is who you are. Own it. Be proud of your talents. Below are some additional examples to help you craft a running list of your own personal talents.

- ➢ **Category:** Living
  - **Example of what could be shared**
    - o *"I can draw."*

- ➢ **Category:** Loving
  - **Example of what could be shared**
    - o *"Would like to begin writing my own message in blank greeting cards for others."*

- ➢ **Category:** Leading
  - **Example of what could be shared**
    - o *"I am patient. Whatever anyone needs, I'm happy to demonstrate."*

- ➢ **Category:** Learning
  - **Example of what could be shared**
    - o *"I would like to improve my annotating skills so I don't have to keep referring to the original text, which is difficult to understand."*

Now it's your turn.

TALENTS

LIVING Authentically, Out Loud!

LOVING Authentically, Out Loud!

LEADING Authentically, Out Loud!

LEARNING Authentically, Out Loud!

Why spend so much time breaking everything down? Because it is uncertainty that breeds our fear and self-doubt. And "fear and self-doubt have always been the greatest enemies of human potential." This is according to self-development author Brian Tracey, who is also a motivational speaker. Putting in the time to work through these activities forces individuals to tackle any fears that may exist within the topics we've covered head-on. Even if you have yet to articulate your purpose, any doubt you possess will be countered by the journey you've undertaken to access your most authentic self. Best yet, the results of the activities can be printed and posted where you can view them daily as a reminder.

You know what you are made of now. You know what you bring to the table. You are beginning to realize how complex you are, how multi-faceted, how multi-dimensional.

Wrap Up

So, what have you learned from this journey? Only you can begin to determine that. And let's face it, there are no quick answers. While this short publication—this primer—may be a quick read, what it offers will take time. Perhaps even a number of passes depending on how authentic you want to be with yourself. Depending on your mood. Depending on where you are in your life at the time. But it is a starting point. And not a bad idea to explore before seeking out a coach.

Personality tests aren't an exact science but for some they can be an interesting place to begin. Maybe the results confirm things already known or they illuminate other aspects otherwise unrecognized. I feel the same about the strengths assessment, especially if you're wrestling with résumés or trying to determine a path. Regardless, we all need to know who that person is staring back at us in the mirror. Once that is known, it's easier to find your true purpose. When life takes on new meaning, when you're no longer swayed by what others say or social media dictates, that is when transformation occurs. And even though you may view things differently than those around you, you won't care because you will be operating from your most authentic self.

Your future is unwritten. You truly do possess the power to be, do, have, and give more. It seems strange only because we have been taught to give up that power in nearly every situation in which we are involved. Not anymore.

Working through the activities, if taken seriously, will not be easy. It's not easy to be honest with ourselves. And following through on what's been suggested will take some time. After all, we are human. We have feelings. We get hurt. We get offended. Egos become bruised. Some of us wear our hearts on our sleeve. We try hard to please others or to look good. Change. Takes. Time. But we can't keep putting everyone else before ourselves at the expense of our own authentic pursuits. Remember, I am not talking about being selfish here. There are those around us who are determined to never grow, evolve, or learn from their experiences. That's not our fault and we no longer need to apologize for things that are not our fault. We can no longer ignore our own self-worth, respect, sanity, and happiness tolerating toxic relationships or situations. It is unhealthy. It is unnecessary. And it is what distracts us not just from following our authentic purpose, but being authentic at all.

Everything starts with you at your most authentic. So, what steps are next? Perhaps most importantly, who are you? At the end of all this, who are you, really?

Gather your thoughts about what's next. What does living authentically look like to you now? What will it look like later in your life? What do you want it to look like? How will you gauge progress as you work on your approach to an authentic life? As you work on a mindset of authenticity, gratitude, and growth?

MOVING FORWARD: YOUR THOUGHTS

GROWTH
ACTIVITIES

MIND MAPPING

Mind Mapping is a powerful tool. We tend to remember things best when they are visual. Mind Mapping's strength is that it taps into both sides of our brain because it is a collection of words, colors, lines, and images.

If you've never done a mind map before, a mind map can identify how you—and perhaps how you think others—perceive you. Consider creating one that reflects your characteristics, or one that details your goals and aspirations—a map not just of who you are, but of who you aspire to be. Mind Mapping can help you to focus on your goals, dreams, and aspirations. It can also help you to develop your sense of self via visualizing the steps needed to grow, develop, and progress.

Observe the example on the next page and then commit to creating a mind-map that encompasses who you are. Have fun with it.

Tap into your inner child. Make it colorful so the various parts stand out. Use crayons, markers, or colored pencils. Cut out pictures from magazines or newspapers. Do it digitally.

Consider making other Mind Maps of the following:

- Your wants, needs, and aspirations

- How you *want* others to perceive you vs how you *think* you are perceived

- Your plan for living, loving, leading, and learning

- Your strengths, skills, achievements, and talents.

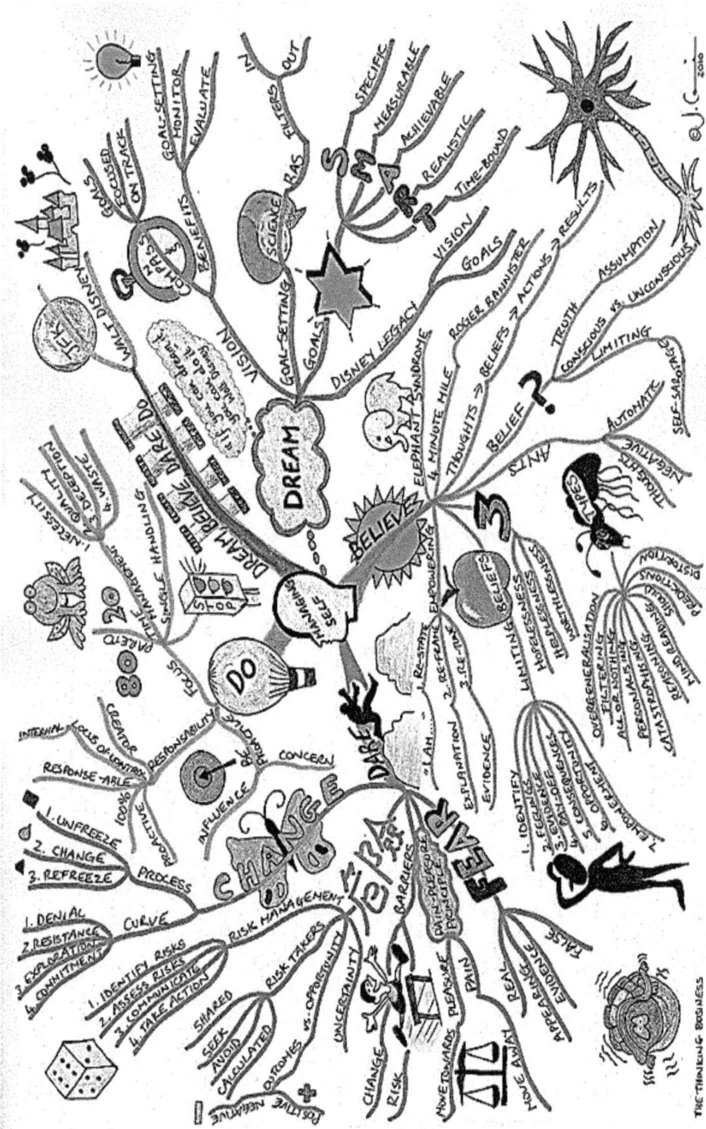
MANAGING SELF
DREAM
BELIEVE
DO
DARE
CHANGE
FEAR
DREAM BELIEVE DARE DO
WALT DISNEY
JFK
VISION
GOAL-SETTING
GOALS
DISNEY LEGACY
COMPASS
GOALS
FOCUSED ON TRACK
GOAL-SETTING
MONITOR
EVALUATE
BENEFITS
SCIENCE
RAS
FILTERS
IN
OUT
SPECIFIC
MEASURABLE
ACHIEVABLE
REALISTIC
TIME-BOUND
VISION
GOALS
ELEPHANT SYNDROME
4 MINUTE MILE
ROGER BANNISTER
THOUGHTS → BELIEFS → ACTIONS → RESULTS
BELIEF ?
TRUTH
ASSUMPTION
CONSCIOUS VS. UNCONSCIOUS
LIMITING
AUTOMATE
SELF-SABOTAGE
ANTS
NEGATIVE
THOUGHTS
TYPES
OVERGENERALISATION
FILTERING
ALL OR NOTHING
PERSONALISING
CATASTROPHISING
MIND READING
PREDICTIONS
DISTORTION
EMPOWERING
BELIEFS
LIMITING
HOPELESSNESS
HELPLESSNESS
WORTHLESSNESS
"I AM..."
1. RE-STATE
2. RE-FRAME
3. RE-TIE
EXPLANATION
EVIDENCE
1. IDENTIFY
2. FEELINGS
3. EVIDENCE
4. CONSEQUENCES
5. OPPORTUNITY
6. EMPOWERMENT
7. EMPOWERMENT
STOP
TIME MANAGEMENT
SINGLE HANDLING
80 20
PARETO
1. NECESSITY
2. QUALITY
3. DECEPTION
4. WASTE
FOCUS
RESPONSABILITY
INTERNAL
LOCUS OF CONTROL
CREATOR
RESPONSE-ABLE
100%
PROACTIVE
INFLUENCE
CONCERN
BE PROACTIVE
1. UNFREEZE
2. CHANGE
3. REFREEZE
PROCESS
CURVE
1. DENIAL
2. RESISTANCE
3. EXPLORATION
4. COMMITMENT
RISK MANAGEMENT
1. IDENTIFY RISKS
2. ASSESS RISKS
3. COMMUNICATE
4. TAKE ACTION
RISK TAKERS
SHARED
SEEK
AVOID
CALCULATED
OUTCOMES
VS. OPPORTUNITY
UNCERTAINTY
POSITIVE NEGATIVE
BARRIERS
CHANGE
RISK
PAIN-PLEASURE PRINCIPLE
PLEASURE
PAIN
MOVE TOWARDS
MOVE AWAY
REAL
APPEARING
EVIDENCE
FALSE
THE THINKING BUSINESS
©J.C. 2010

"I AM"

Another way to access deeper parts of who you are is to work through the "I AM" exercise. Some view it as poetry since it is structured like a Free Verse poem. Regardless of form, the response to each of the opening lines is mind-blowing because of how much it reveals about a person. Take your time with the exercise. Take each line seriously. When done, either print it or write it out for framing. Consider hanging this where you can view it regularly. It's powerful stuff.

I AM... Finish this line with two special characteristics that describe you.

I WONDER... Finish with something you're curious about.

I HEAR... What is it that you hear when you close your eyes? Maybe it's something you hear in your head or around you. Perhaps it is something only you notice.

I SEE... What is it that you catch yourself always seeing/noticing? Maybe it is something others do not see.

I WANT... If given the opportunity, what is it that you'd like? That you want?

I PRETEND... What is it that you pretend (or sometimes pretend) to do?

I FEEL... Emotionally or physically, what is it that you feel or are feeling at this moment?

I WORRY... What is something you worry about?

I UNDERSTAND... Given your life experiences, share something only YOU understand about life. People. Yourself.

I DREAM... What do you dream about? What do you dream of?

I TRY... What is it that you make an effort to do on a regular basis?

I HOPE... What is it that you hope for? This can be about anything.

I AM... Finish this line with the same two special characteristics listed in the first line.

UNLOCKING YOUR LIFE'S PURPOSE[1]

In accessing your most authentic self, the understanding of your purpose should begin taking shape. You can, however, always take what you've learned to the next level by working with a life coach if you are still struggling to determine your purpose. If that's not an option, Adam Sicinski, a life coach out of Melbourne, Australia, has a series of 70 questions as part of a process he calls **The Six Pillars** for determining purpose.

To help you articulate your life's purpose, all 70 questions can be viewed on the following pages. For further guidance, explanations, and additional self-growth resources, be sure to visit Adam Sicinski's website: https://blog.iqmatrix.com/life-purpose.

---

[1] The info on the Five Pillars is taken directly from IQ Matrix Blog.

PILLAR 1: SELF-AWARENESS

Below are questions meant to reveal deeper insights about yourself, such as your strengths, weaknesses, and how others may perceive you.

- What am I meant to do in this world?
- Where have I found real purpose in living?
- What did I want to be when I was a child?
- Which of my traits and attributes seem to stand out most?
- What are my talents and natural abilities?
- Where do my core strengths lie?
- Where am I most effective, efficient, and productive?
- What are my three key weaknesses?
- Where do I struggle most in life?
- What kind of life roles do I enjoy living?
- Which roles do I feel are best suited to my core strengths?
- What life roles just don't suit me at all?
- How would a good friend describe what I am like?
- What do others say that I am meant to do with my life? What is my family's historical legacy?
- What part do I want to play in this legacy?

PILLAR 2: MOTIVATIONS

Answer the questions below to reveal the internal motivations responsible for your behavior.

- What are my passions?

- What would I struggle to let go of?

- Where do I find most inspiration?

- What causes am I most passionate about?

- With a year to live, what would I focus on?

- What three things do I look forward to doing most?

- What three things am I most dreading?

- Where do I like to expend my energy?

- What's been the most satisfying thing I've ever done?

- What have I accomplished that I'm most proud of?

- What have I done that I would like to do more often?

- What activities make me feel fully alive and invigorated?

PILLAR 3: DREAMS

These questions are meant to help you tap into your dreams and future ambitions.

- What would I like to do with my life?
- What would I do if I could not fail?
- What dreams would I pursue if I had unlimited potential?
- What specifically would I like to experience?
- What things would I like to learn?
- What types of skills would I like to master?
- How would I like to express my creativity?
- What things would I like to create?
- Which of these things would I regret most not doing?
- What would I regret most if I simply played it safe?

PILLAR 4: LIFETIME EXPERIENCE

What does your lifetime of experience reveal about you?

- What valuable knowledge and skills have I gained at work?
- How is my work and career path intertwined with my destiny?
- What have been my greatest career accomplishments?
- How do I tend to help others who need my assistance?
- What key skills have I picked up that are of most value to me?
- What unique abilities do I have that separate me from others?
- What have all my failures prepared me for?
- How have all my failures been of value? What insights have I gained from them?
- What have all my experiences over a lifetime prepared me for?
- What specific life experiences have had the most meaning?
- What life experiences have shaped my personality and character in the most profound way?
- How can I possibly draw on these experiences to live a happier and more fulfilling life?
- How could I possibly use these experiences to help me accomplish my dreams and aspirations?

PILLAR 5: CREATING AN IDEAL

Give yourself permission to imagine an ideal life. What would it look like?

- What would my ideal life look like?
- What would my ideal lifestyle be like?
- What would my ideal day look like from morning till night? Describe it in detail.
- What would my ideal week, month, and year be like? Describe it in detail.
- Given my passions, experience, and abilities, what career path would be an ideal fit for me?
- What is my ideal job description? Write it down in detail.
- What does my ideal weekly work schedule look like? Describe it in detail.

PILLAR 6: HIGHER CALLING

What does it all mean? These questions are intended to reveal the meaningful reasons for living.

- What kind of people would I like to help?
- What types of issues do I care most about?
- Where could I provide most value to others?
- What individuals or groups do I most identify with?
- How have all my difficulties equipped me to serve others?
- What lasting legacy would I like to leave behind?
- How will the world be a better place because I have lived?
- What do I care about that is bigger than me?
- What problems would I like to solve?
- Given all this, what is my spiritual calling?

**Given what you know now,
what is your one true life's purpose?**

GRATITUDE JOURNALING

A Gratitude Journal is a great way to slow things down enough to notice and appreciate what is happening around you. Big or small, however mundane some things may sound to others, doesn't matter. This is about you. Living a life of intentional thankfulness is a game-changer. Even on the most difficult days, it will be easier to return to a balanced mindset because you will be able to identify things to be grateful for.

If you are still on the fence about journaling, consider the following from various studies conducted on the effects of Gratitude Journals. One study in 2015 revealed a link between gratitude and the quality of sleep. Those who slept better reported a change in their stress levels and negative attitudes. The same year a study was conducted in Australia involving school leaders. Similar to the aforementioned case, those in the study who kept a Gratitude Journal experienced a more balanced emotional equilibrium. They were also more positive and optimistic in their interventions.

Turkish university students were part of a study in 2017. The results revealed a more enthusiastic transition to university life for those who kept a Gratitude Journal.

A 2018 study found individuals were more satisfied with their lives and relationships when they kept Gratitude Journals.

GRATITUDE JOURNAL
Getting Started

- There's no correct way to keep a GJ.

- Consider when, how often, and how long you want to dedicate to journaling. Then stick with it. Modify as needed until you find the proper fit, but try to be consistent.

- Location. Location. Location. Will you be journaling in bed, the kitchen, at work, in a cab? Will you be using a bound journal, notebook, laptop, tablet, phone? Before deciding, check out the "40 Best Gratitude Journal Templates" link on page 137.

- Try to honor the commitment you've made to yourself to complete these faithfully. Bullet your responses if time is short. You can delve deeper on those days when you have more time. But try not to shortchange the time you've promised yourself to do this. It will be worth it.

- This isn't supposed to be a chore or an assignment. The goal is to be reflective and, in doing so, being specific about what you are thankful for and why.

GRATITUDE JOURNAL
Sample Starting Prompts[2]

1. Write down three things that made your day a little better.

2. Write about someone you're incredibly grateful for today and why. Action Step: Once you finish writing about how grateful you are for them, you can also tell them. You don't have to share everything you wrote about them, but imagine how much you could brighten their day by letting them know how grateful you are for the place they hold in your life and how much you appreciate them.

3. What are some things in your life that you look forward to?

4. Write down five (5) personality traits that you're most grateful for.

5. What is a space that brings you peace, contentment, or joy?

6. What is a memory you have that always makes you smile?

---

[2] Taken verbatim from Krista Brown's Gratitude Journal article.

7. Write about a book that has taught you something interesting or inspiring.

8. Write about someone you admire (this could be anyone from an historical figure to a family member to a literary figure).

9. Write about the foods you are most grateful for and why.

10. What physical item in your household are you most grateful for, and what memory or quality makes you cherish that item?

11. List three (3) people you hope you'll see soon and why you enjoy being around them.

12. List three (3) challenging people for you to be around and name at least one (1) quality of theirs that you admire.

13. When was the last time you laughed without being able to stop?

14. What is your favorite part of the day and why?

For further information on Gratitude Journals and additional prompts, visit scienceofpeople.com/gratitude-journal/

VALUABLE LINKS

11 Life Purpose Questionnaires & Quizzes to Take in 2023

Haven't found the right coach yet? Maybe you have but money is tight. Check out this link with various questionnaires to help you discover your life purpose.
LINK: https://blog.iqmatrix.com/life-purpose

40 Best Gratitude Journal Templates (& List Examples)

Per their website: *"Practicing gratitude is essential for your health and well-being. Studies have shown that this activity offers many impressive benefits like better sleep, fewer symptoms of illnesses, and improved happiness. Create your own gratitude journal using a template or a format of your choice."*
LINK: https://templatearchive.com/gratitude-journal/

Clifton Strengths Finder

Per their website: *"You are stronger than you know. Discover and maximize your most powerful natural talents with Top 5 Clifton Strengths." Fee: $19.99*
LINK: https://store.gallup.com/p/en-us/10108/top-5-cliftonstrengths

Jung Personality Test

Per their website: Though not an official Myers and Briggs test, the *"results of this test will tell you how you rank in each of the four categories [Sensation, Intuition, Feeling, and Thinking] and what that specific combination means."*
LINK: onlinepersonalitytests.org/free-jung-personality-test/

Multiple Intelligences Test

Per their website: *"Multiple Intelligences Test is beneficial to understanding your way of thinking and can support your learning potential. That's why the multiple intelligences test for kids is so popular, but it does not mean that adults cannot also benefit from an MI test."*

LINK: mentalup.co/blog/multiple-intelligence-test

NERIS Personality Test

Per their website: *"Learn what really drives, inspires, and worries different personality types, helping you build more meaningful relationships."*

LINK: 16personalities.com/free-personality-test

RIASEC Career Test

Per their website: *"Answer 20 questions about what sort of activities you might enjoy doing. It will then compare your interests with nearly 1,000 job profiles to find the one that most closely matches your personality."*

LINK: onlinepersonalitytests.org/riasec/

WHAT SHOULD I MAJOR IN? College Quiz

The graphics make this a perfect tool for visual learners. Answers to questions will reveal a list of recommended majors.

LINK: goshen.edu/admissions/2022/01/24/ major-quiz/

* All assessments are free unless otherwise noted.

REFERENCES

Branham, Leigh. *The 7 Hidden Reasons Employees Leave: How to Recognize the Subtle Signs and Act Before It's Too Late*. 2nd ed. New York, NY: AMACOM, 2012.

Brown, Krista. "Gratitude Journal: 35 Prompts, Templates, and Ideas to Start." Self-Improvement. Science of People, October 6, 2022. www.scienceofpeople.com/gratitude-journal/.

Chamorro-Premuzic, Tomas. "1 In 5 Business Leaders May Have Psychopathic Tendencies-Here's Why, According to a Psychology Professor." Make It. CNBC, April 9, 2019. https://www.cnbc.com/2019/04/08/the-science-behind-why-so-many-successful-millionaires-are-psychopaths-and-why-it-doesnt-have-to-be-a-bad-thing.html.

Cormie, Jayne. "Managing Self." Showcasing the World's Finest Mind Maps. MindMapArt.com, 2011. indmapart.com/managing-self-mind-map-jayne-cormie/.

Melore, Chris. "No Place Is Sacred: Addicted Americans Use Cell Phones at Weddings, Funerals, on the Toilet!" MOBILE PHONES NEWS, SOCIETY & CULTURE NEWS. Study Finds, November 20,

2021. https://studyfinds.org/cell-phones-
addicted-americanson-the-toilet/.

Nawoj, Allison. "More than One-Quarter of
Managers Said They Weren't Ready to
Lead When They Began Managing Others,
Finds New CareerBuilder Survey." Press
Room. CareerBuilder, March 28, 2011.
https://press.careerbuilder.com/2011-03-
28-More-Than-One-Quarter-of-Managers-
Said-They-Werent-Ready-to-Lead-When-
They-Began-Managing-Others-Finds-New-
CareerBuilder-Survey.

Nordstrom, David Sturt and Todd. "10 Shocking
Workplace Stats You Need to Know."
Careers. Forbes Magazine, March 18,
2018. https://www.forbes.com/sites/
davidsturt/2018/03/08/10-shocking-
workplace-stats-you-need-to-know/?sh=
29780d73f3af.

Sicinski, Adam. "Here Are 70 Questions to Help
You Unlock Your Life's Purpose." IQ
Matrix Blog, December 8, 2018.
https://blog.iqmatrix.com/life-purpose.

*WE ARE PROGRAMMED TO BE POOR. An Eye
Opening Speech by Dr Bruce Lipton.* YouTube
2019. https://www.youtube.com/watch?v
=Qv8k7Et4ss4.

Young, Paul. "Tactical vs. Strategic: Where PMS
Spend Time." ProductCraft by Pendo,
December 9, 2020. productcraft.com/

perspectives/tactical-vs-strategic-where-product-managers-really-spent-their-time-in-2019/.

"Zig Ziglar Quote: 'Far Too Many People Have No Idea of What They Can Do Because All They Have Been Told Is What They Can't Do. They Don't K...".'" Zig Ziglar Quotes. Quotefancy. Accessed 2019. https://quotefancy.com/quote/943357/Zig-Ziglar-Far-too-many-people-have-no-idea-of-what-they-can-do-because-all-they-have.

Maybe the journey
isn't so much about
becoming anything.
Maybe it's about
unbecoming
everything that isn't
really you,
so you can be who
you were meant to
be in the first place.

summersaldana.com

ABOUT THE AUTHOR

A master certified life coach, Ray LeCara Jr dedicates his time helping people of all ages achieve academic and personal success through his Authentic Embassy business.

LeCara has worked with every grade level K-12, in public and private education, in the traditional classroom, and online. He has also taught adults in the corporate environment as an award-winning trainer.

An author, he has published multiple books of fiction, earning accolades for his short stories and novels. He maintains BestFootForwardOnline.org, an educational resource site he created in 2015. It features inspirational and health information for youth, along with learning resources and academic strategies for learners of all ages. The site is an extension of his education-related publications *Best Foot Forward: A Student Success Guide with Life Skills Strategies for the Road Ahead* (2016) and *Essential Study Skills: A Holistic Approach to Learning* (2022).

Married, Ray LeCara Jr resides in Washington state with his wife and their senior Golden Shepherd rescue.